Glendale Library, Arts & Culture Dept.

3 9 0 1 0 0 5 6 8 7 0 5 5 7

CHILDREN'S ROOM

D1792419

NO LONGER PROPERTY OF
GLENDALE LIBRARY,
ARTS & CULTURE DEPT.

Zoom In on Rocks and Minerals

Gems

Andrea Rivera

j 553.8 RIV

abdopublishing.com

Published by Abdo Zoom™, PO Box 398166, Minneapolis, Minnesota 55439. Copyright © 2018 by Abdo Consulting Group, Inc. International copyrights reserved in all countries. No part of this book may be reproduced in any form without written permission from the publisher. Abdo Zoom™ is a trademark and logo of Abdo Consulting Group, Inc.

Printed in the United States of America, North Mankato, Minnesota
012017
092017

THIS BOOK CONTAINS RECYCLED MATERIALS

Cover Photo: Shutterstock Images
Interior Photos: Shutterstock Images, 1, 4, 14; De Agostini/A. Rizzi/Science Source, 5; Budkov Denis/Shutterstock Images, 6; Tonello Photography/Shutterstock Images, 7; Albert Russ/Shutterstock Images, 8; Dra Schwartz/iStockphoto, 9; Ken Tannenbaum/Shutterstock Images, 10; Anastacia Tkachenko/Shutterstock Images, 11; Pann Chucherd/Shutterstock Images, 12–13; iStockphoto, 13; Muellek Josef/Shutterstock Images, 15; Stephen Jingel/Shutterstock Images, 16–17; Millard H. Sharp/Science Source, 17; Calga Acikgoz/Shutterstock Images, 18; Sebastian Janicki/Shutterstock Images, 19; Bjoern Wylezich/Shutterstock Images, 21

Editor: Emily Temple
Series Designer: Madeline Berger
Art Direction: Dorothy Toth

Publisher's Cataloging-in-Publication Data
Names: Rivera, Andrea, author.
Title: Gems / by Andrea Rivera.
Description: Minneapolis, MN : Abdo Zoom, 2018. | Series: Rocks and minerals |
    Includes bibliographical references and index.
Identifiers: LCCN 2017930329 | ISBN 9781532120442 (lib. bdg.) |
    ISBN 9781614797555 (ebook) | ISBN 9781614798118 (Read-to-me ebook)
Subjects: LCSH: Gems--Juvenile literature. | Precious stones--Juvenile literature.
Classification: DDC 553.8--dc23
LC record available at http://lccn.loc.gov/2017930329

Table of Contents

Science 4

Technology. 8

Engineering 10

Art 14

Math 16

Key Stats. 20

Glossary 22

Booklinks 23

Index 24

Science

Gems are special stones. They are strong and beautiful. They are also hard to find. This makes them precious.

People collect gems.
They often use the gems
for jewelry or decoration.

Most gems are **minerals**.
They form in different ways.
Some gems form from **magma**.

Others form inside rocks. Living things can make gems, too.

Technology

Rubies are red gems.

They were used in the first lasers. They can make the red light from laser pointers.

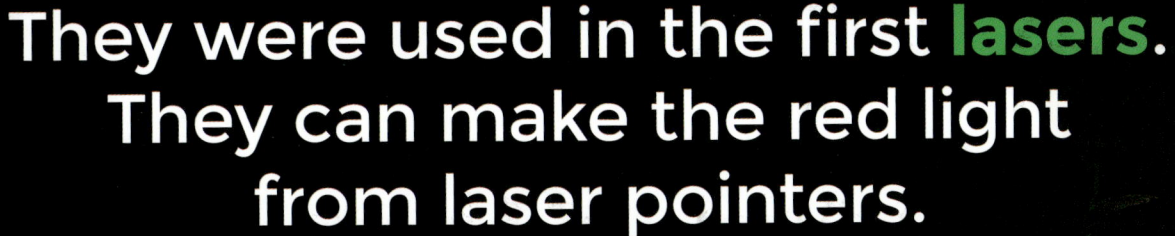

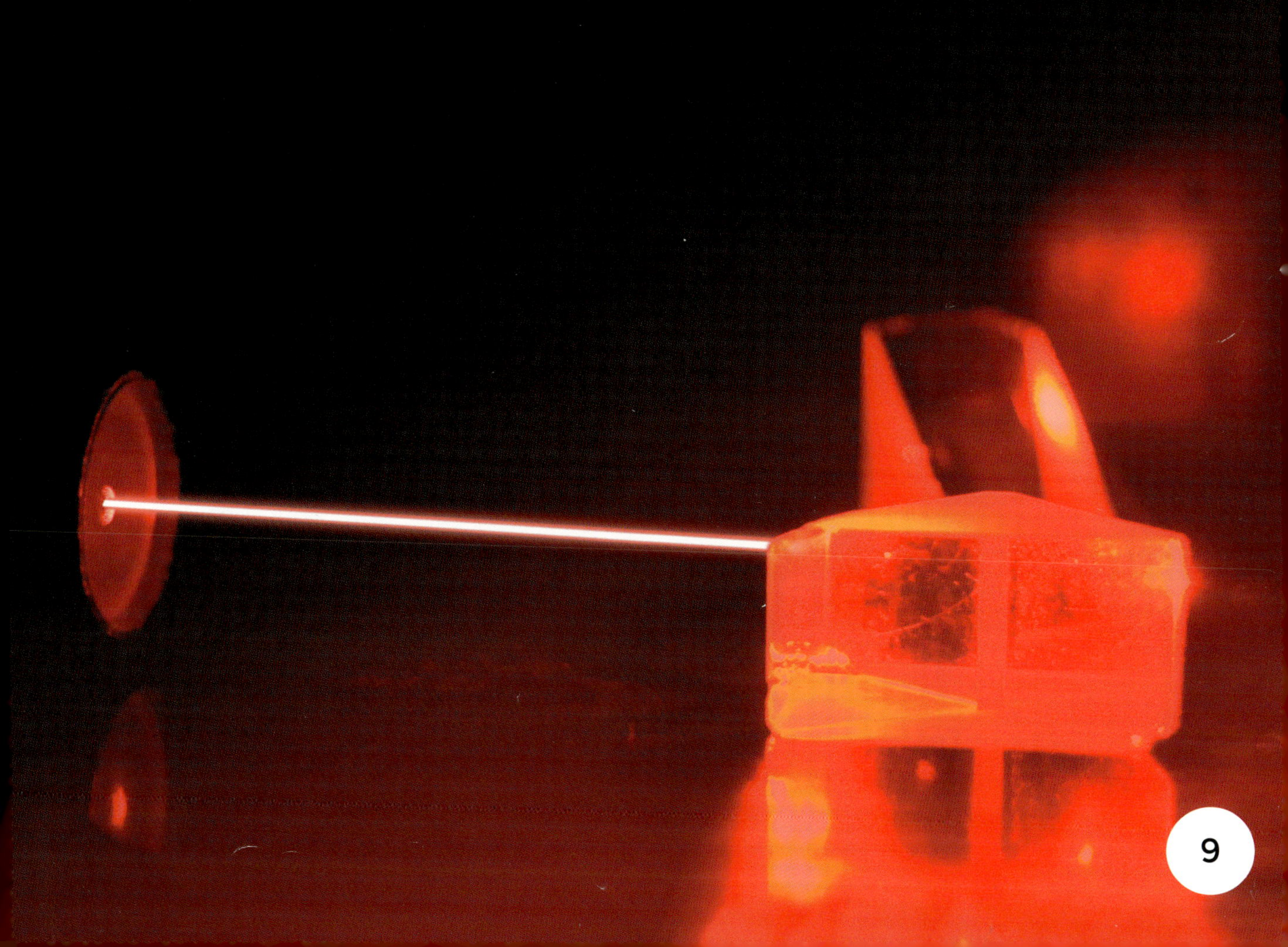

Engineering

Gems are hard. They do not easily scratch or break. Special machines cut them.

Diamonds, rubies, and sapphires are the hardest gems.

Sapphires can be added to glass. They make the glass very strong.

Military vehicles use it for windows. It protects soldiers.

Art

Pearls are used to make jewelry. They form inside oysters.

An object enters the oyster. **Nacre** builds up. It forms a pearl. The pearl is smooth and shiny.

Math

Most gems come from mineral crystals. They grow in six shapes.

Each shape comes from the way its **atoms** are arranged.

The shapes have **faces**.
Some faces look like squares.

Others look like triangles.

- Diamonds form in high temperatures. It has to be more than 2,000°F (1,093°C).

- Some people collect birthstones. Each month is assigned at least one gem. The gems are said to bring good luck to people born during that month.

- Gems have been treasured for thousands of years. Ancient people wore crystals to protect against evil. Some people even crushed and swallowed gems to treat sickness.

Glossary

atoms - the smallest particles. Atoms combine to form molecules.

face - a flat surface that forms the boundary of a crystal.

laser - a device that makes a small, intense beam of light.

magma - very hot, liquid rock from deep inside the earth.

mineral - a substance that forms naturally under the ground.

nacre - a hard, mineral substance.

Booklinks

For more information on gems, please visit abdobooklinks.com

Learn even more with the Abdo Zoom STEAM database. Check out abdozoom.com for more information.

Index

crystals, 16

diamonds, 11

glass, 12

jewelry, 5, 14

lasers, 9

magma, 6

minerals, 4, 16

oysters, 14, 15

pearls, 14, 15

rocks, 7

rubies, 8, 11

sapphires, 11, 12

soldiers, 13